a MERTON
concelebration

WITHDRAWN

W9-BBS-120

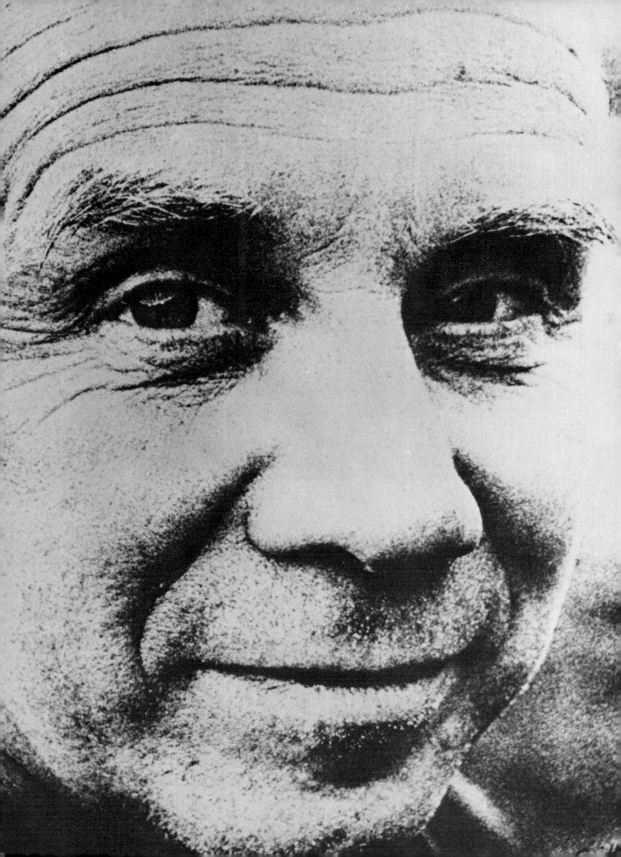

a MERTON concelebration

edited by
Deba Prasad Patnaik
preface by
Brother Patrick Hart

Ave Maria Press · **Notre Dame, Indiana**

Permissions and Credits

Facsimile reproductions for "The Silver Bird . . ." and "The Old Monk . . ." excerpted from COLLECTED POEMS of Thomas Merton. New Directions. © 1977 by the Trustees of the Merton Legacy Trust. Used with permission.

"Edifying Anecdotes Concerning the Deceased Are Now in Order" first appeared in the summer 1969 issue of *Continuum Magazine*. Excerpted from SELECTED AND NEW POEMS by Daniel Berrigan. © 1973 by Daniel Berrigan. Used by permission of Doubleday and Co.

"Tom Merton's Neighbor, Andy Boone, Looks Up" by Jonathan Williams. Excerpted from BLUES & ROOTS RUE & BLUETS. © by Jonathan Williams. Used with permission of Grossman Publishers.

"Death of a Monk (T.M.)" by Mark Van Doren first appeared in *America*. Used with permission of Dorothy Van Doren.

"At Merton's Grave" by Julius Lester first appeared in *The Catholic Worker*. Used with permission of the author.

"Letter to Lancelot" by Francis Sweeney, S.J., first appeared in *Commonweal*. Used with permission of the author.

"Two Poems Dedicated to Thomas Merton" by Jack Kerouac. Used with permission of The Sterling Lord Agency, Inc.

"The Monk Whispers" by Miguel Grinberg first appeared in *Mele*. Used with permission of the author.

"Thomas Merton, Gethsemani, April 1, 1980" by Michael Mott first appeared in *Adena*. Used with permission of the author.

"Connections" by Allen De Loach first appeared in *Poetry Review*. Used with permission of the author.

"To Tom Gone" by Ron Seitz first appeared in *US Catholic*. Used with permission of the author.

"Right After" by Vintila Horia first appeared in *Mele*. Used with permission of the author.

"For Thomas Merton: Lines from a Song" by Joan Baez. © 1976 Chandos Music (ASCAP). Reprinted by permission.

"Tom Merton" by Brother Patrick Ryan, first appeared in *Sisters Today*. Used by permission of the author.

"Death of Thomas Merton" by Ernesto Cardenal (Pring-Mill translation). Used with permission of Search Press Ltd.

International Standard Book Number: 0-87793-238-7

Library of Congress Catalog Card Number: 81-68819

Printed and bound in the United States of America.

Cover and text design: Carol A. Robak

for Annya

Acknowledgments

I wish to thank the Thomas Merton Legacy Trust and its administrator Mrs. Anne McCormick, and Dr. Robert Daggy, Curator of the Thomas Merton Studies Center at Bellarmine College in Louisville, Kentucky, for their cooperation and permission to use Merton materials.

I am much obliged to Mrs. Piedy Griffin for the use of two photos by her late husband, John Howard Griffin.

Brother Patrick Hart of the Abbey of Gethsemani continues to be most kind and supportive. I am particularly thankful for his Preface to this volume.

My editor, Frank Cunningham, has been enthusiastic and helpful.

I express my profound sense of gratitude to all the contributors, translators and friends like Sister Emmanuel, Professor Robert Pring-Mill, Thomas Colchie, Father Daniel Berrigan, Wendell Berry and Jonathan Green for their help.

Contents

Preface

A poetic tribute celebrating the memory of a poet-monk, undoubtedly one of the best known and most beloved of poet-monks, is an appropriate way to commemorate the life and death of Thomas Merton. Certainly he was one who loved life and celebrated it every day of his 53 years. The editor, Indian-born Deba Patnaik, and the other poet-contributors of this volume are for the most part well-known, and many were personal friends of Thomas Merton. What a joy to see them all present here!

Thomas Merton's poetry, now available in the mammoth *Collected Poems* (over a thousand pages!) bears witness to his lifelong need, both spiritual and psychological, to express himself in poetry and poetic prose in an effort to articulate the ineffable, the inexpressible. In this, he was a poet of necessity, a poet with a sense of urgency. Writing poetry was as natural to him as breathing. Not only did he write poems celebrating the seasons of the liturgical year, the contemplative life, social concerns, prophetic voices of the past and the present, and the unity and beauty of all creation, but he read avidly the poetry of others, from the early Irish hermit poets to the Latin American poets of social protest, from the terse and witty Chuang Tzu to the concrete poetry of Robert Lax.

The editor of this volume is to be congratulated for his tireless efforts in contacting poets and friends of Thomas Merton from all over the world. Poets from the East and West, the North and South are represented here, and that is as it should be. It is especially fitting that the volume opens with "Death of a Monk (T.M.)" by Mark Van Doren, Merton's mentor at Columbia University both as an undergraduate and as a graduate student. Their friendship was to last throughout their lives, and it was due in large measure to Van Doren's en-

11

couragement and intervention that Merton's first volume of poetry *(Thirty Poems)* was published by New Directions. When the *Selected Poems of Thomas Merton* was being prepared for publication, it was once again his old Columbia professor who helped in the final choice of poems and wrote an excellent introduction. Van Doren reflects on the death of his friend:

> The best bottle of the best wine
> Tipped over all at once and spilled—
> Catch it, save it, but nobody
> Could. Nothing left but the fragrance . . . .

The present collection has caught some of that fragrance, and now here it is for all who are sensitive to its aroma.

One of the shortest tributes is a concrete poem by a most unusual poet, Robert Lax, Merton's friend from student days at Columbia who now lives in self-imposed exile on one or another of the Greek isles—Kalymnos, Patmos or Lipsos. He speaks of the uniqueness of Merton with the barest minimum of words:

> Singular Star
> Singular Cloud
> Singular Hill . . .
>
> One Hill
> One Cloud
> One Star

The longest poem in this collection is Ernesto Cardenal's "Death of Thomas Merton." Cardenal, now Minister of Culture for the new government of Nicaragua, was a novice at Gethsemani in the late '50s when Merton was Master of Novices. He concludes his verses with:

> We only love and only are on dying
> The final deed the gift of all one's being
> okay

What a congenial group of poet-friends are gathered here—each one adding his or her voice to the chorus. Although there are more men than women represented, the high quality of the feminine voices makes up abundantly for the lack of quantity. Among others there are Joan Baez and Sister Thérèse Lentfoehr (both are poets and musicians), devoted friends of Merton and visitors to the hermitage during his lifetime. Since Merton's death Joan Baez has set his well-known poem "For My Brother Reported Missing in Action" to music (for voice and guitar). The haunting accompaniment resembles the three bells of Gethsemani's church alongside of which Merton lies buried in his Army-issue coffin. She calls the song "The Bells of Gethsemani," and the poignant last lines still resound in my ears:

> The silence of whose tears shall fall
> like bells upon your alien tomb.
> Hear them and come: they call you home.

Baez did some paraphrasing of Merton's poem at the end of the song, adding "And the children are ringing the bells of Gethsemani."

Father Daniel Berrigan in his "Edifying Anecdotes Concerning the Deceased Are Now in Order" recounts the heart-rending "rite of roses"—six roses expressing love and concern for a lonely woman. Lexington poet Jonathan Greene recalls his visits to Merton, leaving with his arms full of books and translations of René Char and the promise of a postcard from Tahiti which never arrived.

And Miguel Grinberg, the Argentine poet, hears the monk whispering, "a thunderclap in the afternoon." Two poet-monks are happily present here, too: Father Charles Dumont, a Belgian Cistercian, and Brother Patrick Ryan, an American Trappist. The latter captures Merton's spirit in his opening lines:

> He was a boy
> at heart. He loved early morning
> in his strange afternoons . . . .

Deba Patnaik concludes the tribute with the memorable words:

> Pilgrim, say the word: the journey
> is
> alone.
>
> Monk, beyond rocks, pond, path
> is
> eternity.

A final memory: When I was asked to contribute a preface to this volume I remembered a similar project Merton was engaged in during the last year of his life. He rather suddenly announced that he would edit and publish four issues—spring, summer, fall and winter of 1968—of a journal of avant-garde poetry and prose, and then let it go out of existence.

With such joy and enthusiasm he undertook this work! He contacted poets and friends from all over the world, inviting them to contribute to this short-lived journal which he called *Monks Pond*, named after one of the lakes at Gethsemani along which he loved to walk and read in the afternoons. When sufficient material was gathered for an issue, he began to arrange the layout, choosing photographs and drawings (often his own Zen calligraphies) as graphic dividers to complement the texts. When looking through the manuscript of this volume I was reminded of Merton's own *Monks Pond*. What we have here in Deba Patnaik's poetic tribute is somewhat the same kind of thing—a concelebration which turns out to be a preview, a glimpse of the kingdom. Let's join in the general dance!

— BROTHER PATRICK HART
Monk of Gethsemani

Introduction

Autumn 1981.

Mottled leaves on trees glaze like stained glass. Shadows and echoes among heaps of dried leaves and baring trees.

My mind winds back to the last fall I spent with Thomas Merton in the woods at Gethsemani. Monastery cheese, whole-wheat bread, and wine for a quiet picnic.

We talked of various concerns—personal and general: friendships, nuclear madness, war, violence, Gandhi, the contemporary revival of spiritual consciousness, the Buddhist and Hindu views of life, reality and death, and of imagination and poetry.

He asked me if I would recite some poems of the Indian bard, Rabindranath Tagore, and of other Indian mystics. I did what I could recall and he recited some of his own—"Night-flowering Cactus," "Crusoe," "April," "Elegy for a Monastery Barn," and "Elias—Variations on a Theme." He paused between poems for us to glory in "thy rubies on these autumn trees," and watch flights of determined, noisy ducks "to lagoons in the south they never saw." It suddenly dawned on me, all his poems are but one hymn which has

> one pattern, no more planned,
> No less perfectly planned
> And no more arbitrary
> Than the pattern in the seed, the salt,
> The snow, the cell, the drop of rain.
> (from "Elias—Variations on a Theme")

They have "no particular message."

15

In his writings, Merton emphasizes that "the logic of the poet—the logic of language and experience itself," is organic, ". . . free. Never typical, always individual." Neither poetry nor contemplation is built "out of good intentions." Words, he suggests, not only "exercise a mysterious and vital reactivity among themselves," but the poetic language, as in the case of symbols, deepens and enriches "the *quality* of life itself by bringing man into communion with the vitality and meaning of creativity, love and truth." This is a powerful and recurrent idea in Merton's aesthetics, as for example when he writes about art in *No Man Is an Island* or *The Sign of Jonas*. In an essay on Louis Zukofsky he writes that the poem "discovers a spiritual vitality that lifts it above itself," and leads both the poet and reader "into contradictions and possibilities"—contradictions in the Blakean sense.

His insistence on the dynamics of art/poetry—its vitality, consonances, contradictions and possibilities—is a key to both the aesthetic and contemplative dimensions of Merton's expression and his life. The aesthetic and contemplative interpenetrate and are complementary. In the essay "Poetry and Contemplation," he affirms:

> In actual fact, neither religious nor artistic contemplation should be regarded as "things" which happen or "objects" which one can "have." They belong to the much more mysterious realm of what one "is"—rather "who" one is. Aesthetic intuition is not merely the act of a faculty, it is also a heightening and intensification of our personal identity and being by the perception of our connatural affinity with "Being" in the beauty contemplated.

Aesthetic intuition, according to Merton, both as a means of appreciation and of creative act, is a mode of heightening and intensifying personal identity. To see any kind of polarity in Merton as a monk and a poet would be a grave misunderstanding of the authenticity of his life.

For writing was also his "vocation." "It is what God has given me in order that I might give it back to him," he remarks in the Preface to the *Merton Reader*. Writing

16

demanded the same kind of "complete simplicity and integrity" that his contemplative life required. In *The Sign of Jonas* he says, "writing, far from being an obstacle to spiritual perfection in my own life, has become one of the conditions on which my perfection will depend." Precisely for this integrated sensibility a poem becomes a "sacrament" or a "presence" for him. Merton's poetry celebrates the "mystery of things." Its "ingrained innocence" awakens "possibilities and consonances." The tortured gestures of the apple trees are as much a "part of my prayer" as is "The Picture of a Black Girl with a White Doll," or the "Kandy Express," or the blade of grass which is "an angel singing in a shower of glory." Be it a creeper or an ant, "all creation teaches us some way of prayer," Merton insists. For him there is in all things "an inexhaustible sweetness and purity, a silence, that is a fountain of action and of joy." *A silence that is a fountain of action and of joy.* Thomas Merton's life as a monk and a poet is a witness to life, action, joy and silence.

As Merton evolved from his earlier poetry of traditional diction, meter and symbolist preoccupation, he displayed a remarkable consummation of his life and art, of daring experimentation. His poetry, whether political or religious in theme, developed an austere and crystal voice. It acquired a peculiar strength, subtlety, purity and compassion—"the most vital expression of life of praise and worship."

The ecstasy instilled in and generated by Merton's poetry is his "apostolate." The world is not made for us to think about, Merton believes, but to give "assent" to. His voice of protest is blended with his voice of affirmation, of assent. His poetry does not end with him, rather it moves and expands into another plane of reality, another dimension of existence—into a silence that resonates its own syllables of mystery and understanding—"Beyond 'yes' and beyond 'now.' "

> Greater deaths
> win greater portions

wrote Merton in the poem "The Legacy of Herakleitos." The

poetic tribute contained in this volume vouches for the "portions" Merton's life and death have brought him. What is evident in these poems is the way the poet-monk touched and inspired such diverse people and with what reverence and affection he continues to be treated. Poets from various parts of the world willingly responded to my request to contribute to this volume and I gratefully acknowledge their kindness.

In *Disputed Questions* Merton points out that all great writing is in "some sense revolutionary," and that life itself is revolutionary "because it constantly strives to surpass itself." He uses the word "revolutionary" to mean revolt as defined in his essays on Albert Camus—"Revolt is based on love. . . . It has to be constantly created anew by a renewal of fervor, intelligence and love." In his life and in his writings, in this sense, Merton remains a revolutionary. This is his gift to us.

— DEBA PRASAD PATNAIK

The silver bird is E backwards in cool pond water.

The paper bird is a pale leaf in ~~the far~~ brown eyed water
She lies limp ~~an~~ over the disk or upturned face
An ~~one~~ underneath ~~the~~ sun,
out of this branded disk
Three eyes or knots ~~the~~ look ~~up and~~ out noplace or upward
Through filtered light
~~There~~ There will be no shadow on this ~~paper~~ surface patern.
The limp bird lies in air or water elsewhere.
Cut like a letter
of some language impossible + perfect. Where E in a mirror
~~Itis~~ Says more than everything.
In a water world that is not ~~entirely~~ alien
But infinitely human. it has wood in it
And the wood has been ~~saved~~ loved
And the bird is cut like a letter
                        true
        Both bird + ~~letter~~ are Saviors
Three white knots of wood are branded on the swat surfaces
~~on the~~
And the stones of a paradise city see themselves backward
            certainties
Spelling ~~certainties~~ in frugal water

Mark Van Doren

Death of a Monk (T. M.)

The best bottle of the best wine
Tipped over all at once and spilled—
Catch it, save it, but nobody
Could. Nothing left but the fragrance.

Which remains. Miraculous,
It fills all air, and is sweeter daily;
And sharper, for this merry mind
Had knives in it, had indignation.

Which could not kill the kindness, did not
Dim the holy brightness—or
We thought it holy; otherwise
How came his wit was never weary?

At Merton's Grave

(for Bro. Patrick Hart and W. Brown Morton)

Behind the chapel is the monks' cemetery.
Like lilies, the white crosses stand,
their arms wide in welcome. The
Cistercian silence is eternal here and
to its currents
Merton would bring his word-scarred soul.
(Sometimes, God can more easily
hold us,
if we walk among the dead.)

Now, he
lies here
where the land begins a slow descent
from the chapel-crested hill.
A benediction-giving cross
marks his Silence
and blesses him, but one must
look on many crosses before
finding his name,
for he was only a monk,
as silent as the grass on his grave
where a brown rabbit nibbled
before Compline

this August evening.

Armindo Trevisan

Elegy for Thomas Merton

He came for you who were barely green to foxes,
knowing your wine would intoxicate
the blood of those on the left:
those you harvested from shadows,
planting at their feet whatever seeds not
devoured by fowl, choked by thorns.

A seaconch to your ear,
always mindful of cries from the abyss;
you penetrated the heart of darkness,
distributed your dog's barking
to those still seated in doorways,
awaiting an Angel's annunciation.

You gathered those idlers to the silence of a hilltop,
where stars hung low,
frogs strummed insane guitars.
There, your fire
consumed the paschal sacrifices,
and, like woman's hair,
engulfed the illumined monastery.

Hares opened each door to your mornings.
Birds, perched in the tower,
their heads underwinged,
announced the thief's arrival:

23

he found you at supper,
the bread already broken,
and your bones aflame with wine.

Translated by Thomas Colchie

Francis Sweeney, SJ

Letter to Lancelot

(For Thomas Merton)

Yes.
The morning has its syllogisms too,
The logic of sunlight antiphonal to the premise.
Greedy of life the little pigs suckle the recumbent sow,
While the jigsawed conifers ponder unruffled,
The young oaks stacked upon the wind.

Majestic the guileless morning, as brightly habited as a
bankrupt
Beyond the fall of dice and the doom of lottery,
Visits his rolling diocese, the great ring unwinking,
Careless of our woe, of the ache in the gullet,
Unembarrassed by the paper prayers burned in the
astrologer's joss-house.

I have heard the white monks singing in the taperlight
Before the rumor of day.
And the cave where I played sleep's witless horrors and
pursuits
Was filled with the morning-color.
The roads that ran in skeins, the mazes without laughter
Are straight as abacus wires.
I have taken the king's shilling,
I have pawned my lute and my knife and the shell of
Compostella;

The bitten, the nitched, the counterfeit sixpence I wager
For a chance of a golden guinea.
Oh lamb-world blind in thickets,
Dear as my blood and the red heart's leather!
The morning, yes.

Two Poems Dedicated
to Thomas Merton

I

It's not that
everybody's trying
  to get into the act,
as Jimmy Durante
says——it's that
EVERYBODY *IS*
    IN THE ACT
        (from the point
            of view of
            Universality)

        Rhymes
            With
                Durante

II

Not oft
        the snow
                so soft
                        the holy bow

27

a few are
    riding
the rest have been
    run over.
            thoreau

James Nicholas

Thomas Merton

Yr oedd yn wr y weddi, — a mynnodd
   Y mynach roi inni
O'r mudandod, gan godi
Llais y nef er ein illes ni.

(He was a man of prayer. The monk,
out of his self-inflicted silence,
insisted on sharing.
He raised for our benefit
the voice of heaven)

*A free translation of the Englyn by the
author. The Englyn is one of the
twenty-four ancient strict meters of
Welsh poetry.*

31

Elza Bebianno

A Page from My Journal:
Thomas Merton
December 1968

Now he is dead,
no need to write the letter—
to say how I admired his words,
how deep his THOUGHT stirred me.

Once I told him, I did not know
what to do with myself after reading
him in the silence of my closed room.
So I let go the book;
time passed, I did not have
the courage to reopen the book.

Now he is dead,
one by one I gather his words,
as if they were ashes of a friend
I never met.
The only one who knew how to say
what I sensed not too clearly.

Now he is dead,
I think of the picture,
he sent me last year.
I see in his eyes

no fear, no lack of certitude
or confidence.
The eyes smile faintly;
in those folded arms, his being
has something of a challenge.

I ask myself,
what could this man go seeking in Far East,
reversing Morning Star's way,
and of the three Wise Men.

Translated by Sister Emmanuel
Deba Prasad Patnaik

Gopal Honnalgere

The Chlorophyl of Silence
—*for Thomas Merton*—

the bodhi tree grows naturally in the garden
some of its branches are long
some of its branches are short
the chlorophyl of its silence
is the wisdom of buddha
                    the tree gives out oxygen
a man should learn to take
a brisk morning walk
not toward his ideal image
but deep into himself
a brisk walk will increase
oxygen in his blood
and his mind becomes very quiet
then he can watch the whole day
his chattering mind
and see that the words
are just a tussle
not to express
but to regain primal silence

Solemn Assizes

Robert Lax

A Poem For Thomas Merton

SIN
GU
LAR

STAR

SIN
GU
LAR

CLOUD

SIN
GU
LAR

HILL

SIN
GU
LAR

CLOUD

SIN
GU
LAR

STAR

SIN
GU
LAR

HILL

ONE
CLOUD

ONE
STAR

ONE
HILL

ONE
HILL

ONE
CLOUD

ONE
STAR

Miguel Grinberg

The Monk Whispers

There was a thunderclap in the afternoon.
There were crystals of tears in a mouth.
No one else in the city heard
the wind among the irons,
the groan in the tongue.
No one but the brother and the stone.

Far away, there up above,
where man and earth join
in a rain of dawns,
there, nowhere else, spaces sing,
invisible seeds flourish,
become murmurs
in farmer's furrows.
There, voices of silence
hold conversations with night.

The monk meditates
by the table in the cell.
Nothing disturbs his tranquil eyes'
caravan of lights.
There is something like music and a toast
in the fibers of his body.

Suddenly his voice whispers:
Blessed are the sowers—
they don't die.

Blessed are the creators;
though they leave, they are
never silent.

In nearby lake, a swan
flaps its wings. The monk slumbers.

In the city, dreams promenade.

Translated by Deba Prasad Patnaik

Carmen De Mello

Sign of Light,
In Memory of Thomas Merton

Another Age,
by your advent.
You arrived on the exact day
to other lights' surprise.
As if in the shattering of unknown nebula,
your Star were a prophetic apparition—
shower of its news-bearing radiance.

Your coming raised a new zodiac mansion,
constellated a spiritual sky.
Clime of your message
created reflective surroundings;
in good time, unfolded the urgent,
new light of your fame, *Merton.*

In your blaze was born our innermost universe
within the constellated space.
Astounding 'alpha' moved into seeming swirl
of other abodes of the Spirit—
cosmological space,
radiant houses of Vega and Aldebaran.

Then our world let go
of its old baggage—

a bankrupt load in the face of sufficiency,
on its new journey.
Your radiance undeflectable.

Eager humanity rushed out
from every nook of christian earth
in the wake of your nova.
Pre-destined sky, entranced by its Cross of Stars,
led a joyous multitude.
This Brazil you loved,
(remember your letters?),
singularly breathed your dawn;
zodiac of the Spirit rose by your rays.

To us, you are a new Epoch
upon sluggish trudge of this century.
A nation of poets leaf through
your joyous calendar
spelt in lyric prophecy.
They open their eyes amazed,
exalt your gifts—
the essence of your poetry
for man and God—
enthralling honor of your Sign of Light.

Translated by Pontes de Paula Lima
Deba Prasad Patnaik

Joel P. Mirabueno

In Memoriam
Frater M. Louis Merton, OCSO

Your head,
O searcher of Truth,
was a bodhi tree
basking in enlightenment,
bearing fruits of toil,
dispersing seeds of contemplation
upon earth hungry for Truth!

Your heart,
O lover of Solitude,
was a hermitage
where you slak'd
your lonely thirsts
with nectar flowing
from the wild flower,
the amaranth of Solitude!

Your hands,
O hunter of Peace,
were dovecots from whence
you scatter'd
throughout the world
millions of pigeons
bringing olive twigs
for seekers of Peace!

Out of a Cloud

(In Memory of Thomas Merton)

Sagittarius spells the first year
of our diminishment
remembering an acre of crosses,
new-turned Kentucky clay
and out of an invisible cloud
the small white hail in a shower—

the last giveaway of his secret
who sat with God in a cloud
and told how it was to be startled
into love. Whether he waded
up the oak-shelved path mixing Stravinsky
and plainsong, or sang with

the Beatles in the cabin on the hill
it did not trouble the cloud.
Paradox of monk who from a hermitage
of a thousand windows
watched our world (loving it) and chose it
his *ashram.* At the sign

of the Lotus he flew oceans
to orient mountains
and there came barefoot to the Burning Bush.
The myth of his cloud
was fire. And home over the shouting
Pacific a gentle sky

had him—a silent guest in the belly
of the jet with his much-
mourned Vietnam brothers (each in his gray
catacomb). In this *now* day
of resurrection, these with him we
celebrate, praising

the Creator who in so brief and
desperate a season
shaped us a friend who reached into our
solitudes and with
the finger of a word touched in us the deep
places of the living God.

Michael Mott

Thomas Merton,
Gethsemani, April 1, 1980

The crippled brother thumps his mattock in
Under the cedar roots where periwinkle grew
Until last night, when wind closed everything.

Our Spring runs backwards from the Easter Hours
To that December Vespers when they buried you
And on your alien coffin different snowflakes fell.

Charles Dumont

What Is Your Face?

*(In Memory of Thomas Merton, my Brother Louis
who has disappeared.)*

You are not just anyone
in the obliterated world.
For whom the bells toll
over your buried body?

The wind identifies you
fleeing into the birches.
Love sacrifices you,
consenting as the water.

In woolen robe,
the *koan* of your name
still wanders over the plains,
where you murmured: "No!"

The humble, holy refusal
thirsting for amplitude
inside its case,
pearled with empty plenitude.

Bangkok, Gethsemani.
Profound soul, monk,
where are you, my friend?
You are not of this world.

Dreamer of solitude.
Dreamer of lofty attention.
Yet, for the multitude,
wounded by compassion.

Pure-hearted, clear-visioned
conqueror of great storms,
will you be in the lightning,
and destroy our blighted shore?

Hermit of the open heart,
you composed your dreams
to nullify grievous lies.

Remember the book, secretly
written of the pain of living,
of Jonas, and of your cries.

Tell us again, your
dazzling dream's hope,
and the march in silence
to your final YES.

Where in the sky are you?
I hear a songbird singing.
Your purest humor,
is it playing with the gospel's 'Pearl'?

Self-effacing prophet, Thomas Louis,
What is your face
in the long summer's gold?

Translated by Deba Prasad Patnaik

Sister Mary Anthony Barr, OP

Enoch

In Memory of Thomas Merton
"Look how fast I dress myself in fire!"

The dark lightning felt your breast like a lover.
And the bells, contrary to legend, summoned thunder.
The Christ of the burnt men seared your heart with
His hand, signed you with His sign: cruz, croaz, crux;
And you, like the flaming monk's palm pinned up to
A desert sky, ascended through sparks into ash;
And thence into glory: the epektesis, at last.
Sweet Christ, how terribly his beauty burns us now!

One sermon more, and there is no more story.
So you disappear.
And the bells, as you predicted, like bridegrooms
Embrace you, filling the echoing dark with
Love and fear.

They have planted you under a cedar tree.
They will think it in future the bodhi tree.
Meanwhile, in realms beyond thought, our
Mentor sits perched (and grinning like a
Gargoyle on the belfry) in his snug Fire
Tower, guarding the abbey and hills;
His, the whole forest of trees.

Allen De Loach

Connections

reflections for Thomas Merton
'found'—hermitage notes of the late John Howard Griffin,
Gethsemani, Kentucky.

'. . . we . . . form part of one same building of living stone. . .'
Merton.

Rain drips steadily into water barrels,
lulls out other sounds
except distant bells from the abbey.

A log fire blazing,
illumines the cabin warmly.

The pop of burning cedar logs,
the blackness of the night:
        a prayer—

    you are just there,
involved in all that,
assenting in wordless amens.

Fragrance of fire.
Charity of logs.

The night & rain & chill & silence,
the woods beyond the walls—
        'Think of it', you wrote,
        'all that speech pouring down,

selling nothing, judging nobody . . .
the talk that rain makes by itself
   all over the ridges. . . .'

A thought:
   Pablo Casals rising every morning,
      Bach Preludes and Fugues
   'to cleanse the atmosphere'—
                     (but no piano here,
                     only the rain).

Solitude—the hermitage—
waking 3:15 a.m.
   A thick ceramic mug, glazed
      (no razor thin china)
   and hot coffee meandering to the belly
   —a wordless prayer—
robust happiness into perceptions.

connections
   The 'rituals', you called them:
      closing windows against cold & rain
      washing the coffee mug, boiling water
         twenty minutes to kill germs
      sweeping straw from hearth to fireplace
         for starting the fire
      sweeping dust from the small chapel,
         fragrance of incense and cedarwood altar
      washing out an undershirt,
         soap-powder promises of 'blazing whiteness
         even in cold water'

      studying, writing,
      caring for the cabin, caring for the body—

flawless only in solitude,
emptied of the junk of self,
paced by rhythms of spirit & body,
   part of nature—& silence & odors & feelings—

Conjoined with your 'Christ of the silences'.

connections

   There is no somberness in this,
   nothing of the 'serious'—
   it handles simply,

   no thing hidden,
   no thing lower than another—
   all are taken up,
      become whole.
             One touch of Nature
               makes the whole world kin.

connections

   The large squirrels outside had thick coats,
      looked fat & sleek—
   no distraction.

connections

   Curious, to speak to you,
   mysterious, a sense of tenderness pervades me,
   persuades.

   And you, Father Louis,
   reciting psalms aloud before dawn,
   & other psalms of no words—

the psalms of stars & clouds
& the wind in trees,
the psalms of coughing
& sneezing & coffee drinking—

an owl hoots in the blanket hush,
these hours before dawn in secret prayer.

'As long as the rain talks I am going to listen', you say.

Charity of logs that consume themselves to warm the room.

Ann Jonas

Three Haikus for Thomas Merton

After the skaters
rice paper   calligraphy
Scribes have come and gone

Their constant squabble
  back and forth over land rights
    Sandpiper and sea.

One little cricket
    winding and winding
        this night into day

Walmir Ayala

The Saint's Hour

In high Tibetan skies,
Merton saw the spark;
saw and tasted deadly rage of the spark.
He perished through love,
crucified in electric star of the spark.

In great noise of steel-ranged mountains
of north-american centers,
the convict sits on a chair,
where flows nervous whip of the spark.

It is the saint's hour.
The great hour of encounters.
Merton in silence gives his last lesson.
In his fingers of protest and grace,
beats the innocent and humble
heart of the spark.

Translated by Luiz Otero

Ron Seitz✝‍ᴧ

To Tom Gone

in memory of
Father Merton

flag your tomb, scarred
the blur of its pitch   humped
      swollen
to what ghost   fainting
      this tongue

crossbone me no victim to that arc
shuttering blind these lids
my mask

but (by   your death twist)
wrinkle this kiss
saint both of us &
holy   the gnaw
      of our chalice

Daniel Berrigan, SJ

Edifying Anecdotes Concerning the Deceased Are Now in Order

January; a sick woman
garnished with the dumb potatoes
of average do-gooders
preserved, propped there
a vinyl-sprayed op exhibit;
Soup Cans, Groceries; "IDEAL SLUM."
(Around her hideous fairy tales arise
in the eyes of the children of good parents
potato parents, canned pops and moms)

Enter Merton.
He stooped and kissed the woman
(she dying not of this ill or that
but of all   all
her life and ours)
offered
six roses
A sudden weeping seized her
drained by average goodness of church and state
their boiled eyes and lives.

Touché, excelling man!
never again shall we
(canned, mashed, boiled
in the short order of creation)
cry out, exult—never again
that rite of roses
that rightness, the rose that leaps
once, and for all
dies

Peregrinatio
(For Thomas Merton)

You leaned against the building
that afternoon, talking,
in city clothes your pockets
crammed with film and credit cards.
We exchanged pleasantries
about the way people
plan trips—nothing more profound—
only that silence was broken
and I saw the joy of speech
spread smiles across your face.

　　　Once, when you were ill you
said, "A little bit of meat, please . . ."

We could have talked of mysteries
the quiddities of faith
while traffic hummed a monotone
down busy avenues—
your words, warm, comic,
I hardly remember—
only the pilgrim eyes, searching,
sighting at last the lost island.

Now I pass the empty doorway
where you stood
wishing I could recall your words
the timbre of your voice—
no matter:
we shared a moment's comfort
from wind and crowd—
a few words out of the silence
men draw about them.

Traveler: for you
a friendly encounter, brief shelter
among many doorways
before your long journey
to the last hostel.

Right After

in Memory of Thomas Merton

No one goes around unpunished.
Certitude leaves no trace.
If you are here, it is not now;
my knowledge fumbles.

I know speed. I do not know
the place it imposes on your journeyings.
The hand rises.
There is no need to travel anymore.
The voice breaks in, does not aver.
It is no longer possible
to engender barbarities with Eros.

Lawyer's reasoning, you cry out,
with your teeth more logical
than the executioner's sword.
Sophists lodged in your blood shout half-truths;
dogs sculpt wit their nippings
my most savoury flesh;
my entrails swing with you.

If I love, there is no answer.
You, not I.
At once in the spirit,
in the senseless flesh.

There is, you say, only one window.
You submit to the laws.
Not to love.
I listen to your speech, your voice of winter.
And with my rags under my arm,
stubborn, I enter the second exile.

Translated by Deba Prasad Patnaik

For Thomas Merton

The Saints all died fools

Simeon fallen thirty-six feet from his tower
into uneven rocks

Francis blind from eating garbage, stigmatized
his order grown beyond him

and you Thomas Merton found burning on wet terrazzo
your demon lover the electric fan still on top
and buzzing you forever at two-twenty
while Eulalia and your mother called
each from her separate pyre.

You were indeed that day the candid bird pursued
en fil-de-fer plumé d'orages and held *à*
l'instant du nerf qui éclate, le bloc sourd de la sensation
as your feet slammed the floor like guns in Gethsemani.

You would have laughed your body sent back a number wired
securely to the right forearm among dead from Vietnam.

You would have roared the poem INVENTORY OF EFFECTS
     ESTATE
OF THOMAS MERTON BANGKOK THAILAND JEWELRY
     HEIRLOOMS ARTICLES
OF SENTIMENTAL VALUE 1 TIMEX Self-Wind Waterproof
Watch with expansible bracelet value ten dollars 1

Pair Dark Glasses in Tortoise Frames value nil 2 Cistercian
Leather-Bound Breviaries value nil 1 Rosary Broken value
nil 1 Small Icon on Wood of Virgin and Child value nil
at your funeral the brothers could not mourn.

Nor will I mourn you

but with these slight words that kill you again
I canonize you Blessed Fool, Burned Father
driven into silence like a nail and beautiful
forever on the borders of outrage.

Joan Baez

For Thomas Merton:
Lines from a Song

But time will pass and so, alas,
will most of what we know. . . .

But I'll play ball with the underdog
and sit with the child
who's wrong.

Be still when the earth is silent
and sing when my strength is gone.

Tom Merton

He was a boy
at heart. He loved early morning
in his strange afternoons.
Weary of this world
                          he split

as a seed
sinks
in soil.

This father leads where
flowers bloom a different
way. So strange

our seed lives.

Tom Merton's Neighbor,
Andy Boone, Looks Up:

Father,

when the wild turkeys
fly south
and say

W

A

R

with their wings,

it's liable to be
war

Jonathan Greene

On Hearing of Merton's Death

Always selfish in loss,
I berate you for dying,
leaving us here
stranded in life.

Our last meeting
I found you
at the monastery gate,
seeing again

not the expected solemnity
your prose suggested,
but a levity
you had come to.

The trials were hidden,
the devotions—private
and singular, as they are
in the end.

Often I kidded:
that I knew many more monkish
than you living in cities,
in the secular.

That night we sneaked
into town for supper
only to be pointed out
to some novice.

I left you by the road
to the hermitage.
You sent books, translations
for Char in a cribbed script.

Your last letter promised
a post card
from Tahiti
that never came.

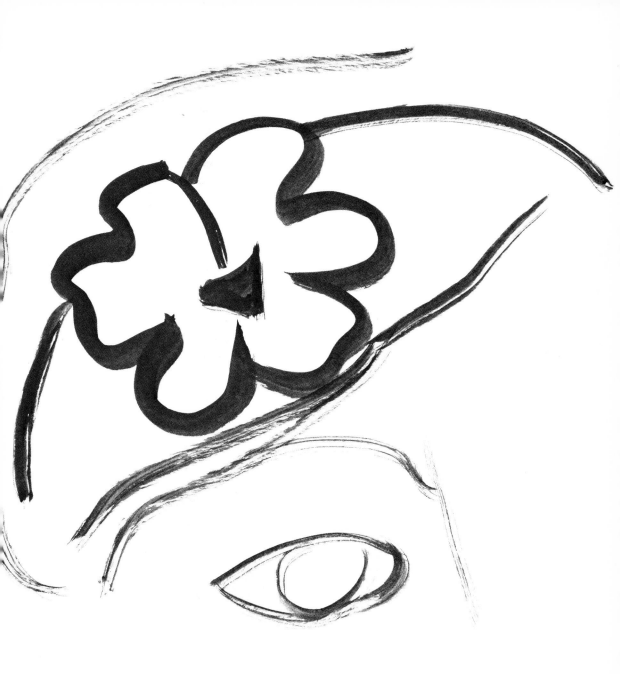

Ernesto Cardenal

Death of Thomas Merton

Manrique said our lives were rivers
going down to the sea which is death
but the death they flow down to is life
And your death was more of a quirk, Merton
                (absurd as a zen koan?)
"Made by General Electric"
and your body flown to the States in an Army plane
      you'd have had a good laugh, given your sense of humour
you Merton bodiless and dying of laughter
likewise myself
The initiates of Dionysus used ivy leaves . . .
        I knew it not:
I tap out this word "death" with joy today
Dying isn't something like a car-smash
              or a short-circuit
   we die throughout life
Contained in our lives—
      like the canker at the apple's core? No
not like the canker but
the ripeness!
Or like mangoes, here in Solentiname, in summer
going slowly yellow, waiting
for the golden orioles . . .
       the hors d'oeuvres
in restaurants were never as good
as in the advertisements

nor the poem as good as we hoped
nor the kiss.
We have always desired more than we lacked
We are Somozas seeking to own ever more haciendas
      More More More
nor yet just more, but something "different"
    The nuptials of desire
The coition of perfect will is the act
of dying.
      We move among things with the air
of having mislaid a most important
briefcase.
       Take escalators up and take them down.
Enter the supermarket or the store,
like anyone else, seeking the transcendental
product.
      We live as though waiting
for an infinite assignation. Or
                 to be called to the phone
by the Ineffable.
And are alone
the grain that does not die, yet are alone.
We sit at ease on deck and dream
    contemplating sea the colour of daiquiri
waiting for someone to pass and smile at us and
say hello.

Not sleep but lucidity.
    Moving like sleepwalkers through the traffic
      past the traffic-lights
eye-open yet asleep
savour a Manhattan as though asleep.
Not sleep but
lucidity is the true image of death
    of its illumination, of the blinding
splendour of death.

Nor is it the Kingdom of Forgetfulness. Memory
        is secretary to forgetfulness.
                She keeps the past in filing cabinets.
But when there is no more future merely an instant present
all that has been lived relives no longer as memories
and reality reveals itself entire
in one flash.

Poetry was a parting too
like death. Full of the
sadness of departing trains or planes
                        the trains which pass in the night
                        through the station of Brenes
                        Cordobita below full of light
cante jondo in the depths of Granada . . .
In all beauty, a sadness
and a longing as in an alien land
                MAKE IT NEW
                ("a new heaven and a new earth")
but beyond this lucidity
the return to cliches, the return
to slogans.
It is only when we are not being practical
and concentrate on useless things that we
move out and find the world is opening out.
Dying is the act of being quite uninvolved
likewise: Contemplation.
Love, love above all, as it were a foretaste
of death
        Kisses had the savour of death in them
                being
                        involves being
                                in some other being
        we only are when we love
But in this life we love only by fits and starts
and weakly

We only love and are when we cease being
when we die
                    a nakedness of being that we may make love
                        make love not war
                    going down to the love
                    which is life

the city come from heaven which is not Atlantic City—
        nor the hereafter an *American way of life*
                            Retirement in Florida
or one long limitless Weekend.
Death is a doorway opening
onto the universe
                    No sign which says NO EXIT
and into ourselves
                                (the journey
        into ourselves—
                not to Tokyo or Bangkok—
                            that is the *appeal*
            "air hostess wearing a kimono,
Continental cuisine"
the real *appeal* of those Japanese Air Lines advertisements)
        A nuptial night, as Novalis put it
Not one of Boris Karloff's horror films
And natural, as is the fall of apples
subject to the law which draws the stars, or lovers
—There are no accidents
            just one more apple off the Tree
you're merely one more apple
Tom
                    We quit the body as one quits
                    a motel room
But you're not Wells's invisible man
                Nor like a ghost in a haunted house
                    We need no *mediums.*
And children knowing that there's really NO thing there

86

that we are immortal
Can napalm blot out life?
                    Does the gas-chamber lead to nothingness?
          Are the Gospels just SF?
Jesus went into the room and put the mourners out
               That is why swans sing said Socrates
just before death
                    Come, Caddo, let us all ascend
                         to the great Village in the sky *(twice)*
—To which all buses and all aircraft go
               Not as to a destination
               but to the Infinite
               We fly towards life at the speed of light
As the foetus bursts the amniotic bag . . .
Or as cosmonauts . . .
                         —the coming forth
                         from the chrysalis

          A *happening.*
the climax
of one's life

                    dies natalis
          of this pre-natal life . . .
The womb of matter left at last behind
                              Not something absurd:
                              but a mystery

a doorway opening onto the universe
not onto the void
          (like the door into an elevator which is not there)
Definitive at last.
          Such is the awakening of one man, one morning,
          at the voice of a nurse in the hospital.
And we no longer have but merely are
          but merely are and are mere being
                    The voice of the lover saying
                    beloved take off your bra
The doorway opening

that no one can now close—
                    "God who bade us live"
much though we may hope to return
        to the first linkage of atoms, to
            unawareness.
                            The bombs get bigger every day.
Necrophilia: flirting with death. The lust for what is dead
            (corpses, machines, money, trash)
and if they dream of a woman she is made
in the image of an automobile
        The irresistible attraction of the inorganic
                Hitler was seen in World War I
                crouched down to view a corpse
                and would not move away
(the military, machines, or money, shit)
Gas-chambers by day and Wagner in the evening
"5 million" said Eichmann (or maybe 6)
Or else we wish to give death beauty treatment
The Loved Ones (do not call them dead)
made-up, manicured, and with a smile
in the Garden of Rest of the Whispering Glades
        cf THE AMERICAN WAY OF DEATH
    one or two martinis to forget his face
relax and watch TV
                        the joy of driving a Porsche
                        (any line you choose)
perhaps to wait for resurrection in deep-freeze
in liquid nitrogen at −197°
    (stored like the grain which never dies)
until the day when immortality comes cheap
After coffee, Benedictine
a sports-jacket to stay young, to keep death off
while waiting for the elixir of youth to be discovered
                    the antidote
to dying.
Like the good cowboy in the films, who never dies.

       Seeking the Fountain of Youth in Miami,
the pleasures advertised in the Virgin Islands
Or sailing Lethe on board Onassis' yacht . . .

You did not seek to be a man who is a Name
whose face is recognized by all who read
the tabloid press
Your wilderness which flowered as the lily
was not Paradise Valley Hotel
          with cocktails served in the pool
beneath the palms
nor were your solitudes those of Lost Island
     with coconut-trees bending towards the sea
LOVE? *It's in the movies*
        the irruptions of eternity
        were brief—
Those of us who disbelieved this world's *Advertisements*
        dinner for two, "je t'adore"
            How to say love in Italian?
You said to me: the
        Gospel never mentions contemplation
No LSD
but the horror of God (or
        should we translate it "terror"?)
        His love like the radiation which touches not yet slays
and a void far greater than the Macrocosm!
        The only vision in your meditation
        that plane on the Miami to Chicago run
        and SAC's plane carrying the Bomb
        the days in which you wrote to me
My life is one of deepening contradiction and frequent darkness
Your *trip*? such a dull one
     a voyage into vast solitudes, expanse of nothingness
all chalklike
        black and white, *with no colour*
a watching the luminous ball, blue and rose like agate

Christmas on Broadway with songs and copulation
shining on the dusty waves of the Sea of Tranquillity
or the Sea of Crisis dead to the harsh horizon. And
like the glinting ball hung on a Christmas tree . . .

       Time? *IS money*
is *Time Magazine,* is a state of boredom, a nothing
      Time with a celebrity depicted on the cover

And that advertisement for Borden's Milk, under the rain
way back at Columbia, switching on
and switching off, only so fleetingly on
             kisses in a cinema
films and film-stars
all so fleeting
        GONE WITH THE WIND
although the dead stars may still smile in their beauty
on the screen
       the car breaks down, the fridge
is sent away to be repaired
           Her dress butter-yellow
            marmalade orange and strawberry pink
like a New Yorker ad imprinted on the memory
lipstick already smeared by kisses
farewells at the windows of planes bound
                     for oblivion
shampoos for girls more distant than the Moon
or Venus
      Eyes more precious than the Stock Exchange
Nixon's inauguration long since past
the last image on the screen dissolved
and the streets of Washington swept clean
Time Alfonso Time? *Is money, mierda, shit*
time is but *The New York Times* and *Time—*
      And all things seemed to me like Coke . . .

Proteins and nucleic acids
   ("how fair the numbers of their forms")
proteins and nucleic acids
   bodies are like gas to the touch
and beauty a bitter gas
like tear-gas
   Because the film of this world passes . . .
     like Coca-Cola
  or copulation *for*
  that matter
Cells are as ephemeral as flowers
     yet life is not
  protoplasm chromosomes yet
life is not
   "We live again" as the Comanches sang
   our lives are the rivers which
   flow down to life
now we see but as on television (darkly)
but later, face to face
    All perception but a trial of death
     beloved this is the pruning season
 The many kisses which you could not give will all be given
    the pomegranates are in bloom
all love but a *rehearsal* of death
   So we fear beauty

When Li Chi was carried off by the Duke of Chin
she wept until her tears had soaked her garments
but when once in the palace she regretted
having wept
  The *San Juan de la* ✠ rounds the headland
   some ducks
   fly over
     "the remote isles"
or "longing" as St. John of the Cross called it
infinite longing

91

       rend the garment of this sweet encounter
the Thracians mourned their births according to Herodotus
and sang their deaths—
It was in Advent, when the apple-trees down by the greenhouse
in Gethsemani are skeletal
and blossom white with frost
like frigidaires . . .
Alfonso in the madhouse said I don't believe it
when I told him that Pallais was dead
it must be politics he said
or something of that sort.
Do they still bury a camel with them
for the journey? and the whale-toothed clubs
with Fiji islanders?
Men's laughter at a joke proves they believe
in resurrection
       or when a child wakes in the night and cries
and his mother soothes him
Evolution is towards more and more life
      and it is irreversible
incompatible with the hypothesis
of the void
Yvy Mara ey
migrations sought it in the heartland of Brazil
("the land of no dying")
    Like mangoes here in summer in Solentiname
ripening
whilst there the whole novitiate is cowled in snow.

     The orioles
       seek out Deer Island where they sleep
you said to me
It is easy for us to approach him
We are strangers in the cosmos tourists really
       having no dwelling here but just hotels
Like Yankee tourists

everywhere
swift with the camera but never really knowing
As one quits a motel room
YANKEE GO HOME
Over Solentiname another evening dies
Tom

these sacred waters glitter
and then go slowly dull
time to light the Coleman
all joy is union
absence of others, pain:
Western Union
The cable from the Abbot of Gethsemani was yellow
WE REGRET TO INFORM YOU etc . . .
and I just said
okay

Where the dead unite and
are with the cosmos
one

"which is far better" (Phil. 1:23)
Just as the moon dies and is reborn . . .
death is union and
one is at last oneself
in union with the world
because death thus is better
the flame-trees bloom tonight, scattering life
(their renunciation is a scarlet flower)
death is union
half-moon over Solentiname
with three men
one does not die alone
(the Great Lodge of Reunion) the Ojibway
and the world is even deeper
Where Algonquin spirits wearing spirit moccasins
hunt beaver spirits over spirit snow
we thought the moon was so far off

93

dying is not to leave the world
but to dive into it
to reach the "alternative" universe
        the *underground*
out of this world's *Establishment*, out of space-time
neither Johnson nor yet Nixon
        there are no tigers there
                        say the Malays
(an Isle in the West)
                which go down to the sea
                which is life
Where the dead are met together oh Netzahualcóyotl
or "Heart of the World"
                Hemingway, Raissa, Barth, Alfonso Cortés
the world is even deeper
                Hades, to which Christ descended
                centre: belly (Matt. 12:40)
                        SIGN OF JONAS
                the depths of all visible beauty
where the great cosmic whale swims on
replete with prophets
                The kisses which you did not give will all be given
Is transformed.
. . . "as one lay buried in one's mother's womb . . ."
                a Cuna headman said to Keeler
Life does not end but is transformed
        another wombed existence say the Koguis
who therefore place their dead in hammocks
in the foetal pose—
                Plato said it was an old belief
that there are people in Hades
                who had come from here . . .
Beziers, the cathedral as one sees it from the train
        Nothing one recalls with yearning is lost
                the scent of the Midi
the red tower of Saint Jacques down by the Tarn

94

lights white and green, in Paris: on the Eiffel
                    Tower: *C-I-T-R-O-E-N*
Lax travelled with circuses
                and knows what it is
to take the Big Top down by lamplight
leave the site bare
and travel in a lorry through the night to another city
And when the wife of Chuang Tzu died
Chuang Tzu did not mourn
          Hui Tzu found him singing and dancing and
using the rice-pan as a drum
        the hammock is the placenta, the hammock's
rope the umbilical cord
          "your headaches will do you no harm"
              seed—plant—seed
         the dialectics of destruction
                I speak
of wheat. Living
is for dying, for giving in the scattering of life
Until the masked and white-gloved coming
of the secret agent
            whose identifying letters are unknown to us
To give ourselves to death with love
And
if the stars die not
each stays alone
if they do not go back to cosmic dust
            seed—plant—seed
death is union
             not in Junction City
Or, as the Cunas likewise say,
         "One day we would like a good dinner"
We clamour for the total giving of the Lover
Or as the Abbot Hesychius said:
Frequent meditation upon death is
"as when fish disport themselves in a quiet sea
and dolphins jump rejoicing"

And, just as the moon dies . . .
            They are on an island, Columbus
    was told in Haiti, together on an island
    eating mameias in the night—
Or, again, the isle *Boluto,* East of Tonga
a place of joy and flowers and spiritual bread-fruit
"apparently electrocuted"
                    Laughlin wrote me
"at least it was over quickly"
                            the tearing of the veil
between the soul and God . . . And:
. . . since love desires the passage should be brief . . .
    the soul's rivers of love
    flow thither to join the sea
arriving lovely as Joan Baez in a big black car
You used to laugh at ads in the New Yorker
    yet here's one by Pan Am
    ***Ticket to Japan*
            To Bangkok
                    To Singapore

    All the way to the mysteries
A ticket for contemplation? Yes
    A ticket for contemplation.
                    Also for death

    All the way to the mysteries
Advertisements are manuals
of meditation, says Corita
                Sister Corita
and advertising something more. Don't take them
at face value.
Biological death: it must be politics
or something of that sort.
    General Electric, fate
        a jet from Vietnam to bear the corpse
but once this winter is over, at Eastertide

96

or Whitsun
you'll hear the Trappist tractors near your cemetery
Trappist yet noisy, fresh furrowing the earth
So as to plant, new Mayas, ancient maize.
—The time of resurrection for the locusts
                and the Caterpillars
Like the banana-tree which dies to produce fruit, Hawaiians say.
                You were empty
                        with all love given, you
had nothing left to give
                        Ready to go to Bangkok
To start the beginning of the new
accept the dying of the old
                        Our lives
                        flowing down to life
on taking off from California
                the windows of the jet wept tears
        of joy!
At last you've reached Solentiname (it wasn't *practical*)
after the Dalai Lama, and Himalayan buses
painted like dragons
                "the remote isles"; you're here
with your silent Tzus and Fus
Kung Tzu, Lao Tzu, Meng Tzu, Tu Fu—and Nicanor Parra—
and in all places; as easy to communicate with you
as it is with God (or just as difficult)
                like the whole cosmos in one drop of dew
this morning on the path to the latrine
Elias taken skyward in a chariot of cosmic energy
        or the Papuan tribe that seeing the telegraph
        made a small model
        to talk with the dead
Valerius Maximus tells us that the Celts
lent money to be repaid beyond the grave.

                All the kisses given or not given.

97

That is why swans sing said Socrates
the fan still whirling
at your heart
              We only love and only are on dying
     The final deed the gift of all one's being
okay

Translated by Robert Pring-Mill

The old monk is turned loose
And can travel!
He's out to see the world.
What progress in the last Thirty years!
But his mode of travel
Is stile the same.

2/18/76

Hard rain fell through the night
and the weather has been warm.
Now, before their time, the pastures
are turning green. The buds
of the water maples have opened;
the light rising against them,
the branches hold a veil of red.
In their coverts the birds
are singing, and there is a veil
of song over the bare branches.
Awake in the night, I heard the wind
heave over the points of the upland.
In the calm morning I heard
geese beyond the river, and looked
to see their raveled V rising
into sight, passing over. I heard
their voices, and thought of no reply.
But the time has come again
to look up from the page, look up
from axe-work or hand-work—the time
of voices traveling in the sky.

Deba Prasad Patnaik

For Thomas Merton

". . . His everlasting secret
Too terrible to bear." Merton

Death
is no secret.
Not even in ambush,
or by an electric fan.

Surely not your death.
There was something
perfect,
whimsical about it.

Maybe, you did not get a chance
to complete your last prayer;
could not say
hallelujah or amen.
How does it matter?

Nothing but the terrible is perhaps
real.

Pilgrim, say the word: the journey
is
alone.

Monk, beyond rocks, pond, path
is
eternity.

Chronology

1915   January 31. Born at Prades, France; son of artist Ruth Jenkins of Zanesville, Ohio, USA, and artist Owen Merton of Christchurch, New Zealand.

1916   Baptized in Prades with Dr. T. Bennett of Harley Street, London, as godfather. Moved to Maryland and New York. Lived with mother's family in Douglaston, Long Island, NY.

1918   Birth of brother John Paul.

1921   Mother's death, of cancer in Bellevue Hospital, NY.

1922   Attended elementary school in Bermuda.

1923   Returned to Douglaston.

1925   Trip to France with father. Residence at St. Antonin.

1926   Entered Lycee Ingres, Montauban, France. Christmas with father and M. & Mme. Privat in Murat, France.

1928   Returned to England.

1929   Entered Oakham School, Rutland, England.

1931   Father's death, of brain tumor. Stayed with godfather Bennett in London.

1932   Graduated from Oakham; scholarship to Clare College, Cambridge University.

1933   Trip to Italy; summer in USA; entered Cambridge in fall to study modern languages (French & Italian) in preparation to get into British Diplomatic Service at Dr. Bennett's insistence.

1934   Gained second in Modern Language Tripos, Part I, at Cambridge. Moved back to New York.

1935   Entered Columbia University in February. Friendship with Professor Mark Van Doren.

1936   Death of Pop—grandfather. Friendship with Robert Lax, Robert Giroux, Ed Rice, Sy Freedgood.

1937   Death of grandmother. At Columbia, editor of 1937 *Yearbook*, art editor of Columbia University *Jester*. Periodic encounters with Raissa Maritain. Winter '37 through early '38 avid reading of Oriental religions and philosophy. Growing interest in spiritual life.

1938   Meeting with Brahmachari. Graduated from Columbia. Began work on M.A. in English. First Sunday Mass at the Church of Corpus Christi, NY. Consulted Fr. Ford for becoming a Catholic. Meeting with Dan Walsh, professor of philosophy at Columbia. November 16, baptism and first communion at Corpus Christi with Ed Rice as godfather, and Lax, Freedgood present. Book reviews for *NY Times*, *NY Herald Tribune*, until 1940.

1939   M.A. from Columbia. Teaching English in University Extension. Teaching at St. Bonaventure University until 1941.

1940   Meeting with Catherine de Hueck (Doherty); went to her Friendship House in Harlem, NY, to work. Trip to Cuba.

1941   Easter, first retreat at Gethsemani at the suggestion of Dan Walsh; decided to join as a monk.

        December 10, entered the Abbey of Gethsemani.

1943   April 17, death of brother John Paul.

1944	March 19, Simple Vows of Cistercian Order. Publication of THIRTY POEMS, New Directions.
1946	A MAN IN THE DIVIDED SEA, New Directions; second volume of poems.
1947	March 19, Solemn Vows.
1948	FIGURES OF AN APOCALYPSE, New Directions; poems. THE SEVEN STOREY MOUNTAIN, Harcourt, Brace; autobiography. EXILE ENDS IN GLORY, Bruce; biography.
1949	May 26, ordained priest at Gethsemani with Van Doren, Lax, Rice, Freedgood present. Golden Book Award by the Catholic Writers Guild of America for THE SEVEN STOREY MOUNTAIN. SEEDS OF CONTEMPLATION, New Directions; religion. THE WATERS OF SILOE, Harcourt, Brace; history. THE TEARS OF THE BLIND LIONS, New Directions; poems.
1950	WHAT ARE THESE WOUNDS?, Bruce; biography.
1951	June 22, American citizenship in Louisville, KY. Master of the Students, Gethsemani, until 1955. St. Francis de Sales Award by the Catholic Writers Guild of America for THE ASCENT TO TRUTH, Harcourt, Brace; theology. THE ASCENT TO TRUTH, Harcourt, Brace; theology.
1953	THE SIGN OF JONAS, Harcourt, Brace; journal. BREAD IN THE WILDERNESS, New Directions; theology.
1954	Meeting with Victor Hammer. THE LAST OF THE FATHERS, Harcourt, Brace; theology.
1955	Master of the Novices until 1965. NO MAN IS AN ISLAND, Harcourt, Brace; religion.

1956   THE LIVING BREAD, Farrar, Straus; theology.
THE STRANGE ISLANDS, New Directions; poems.

1957   Friendship with Ernesto Cardenal as a novice at
Gethsemani. Trip to St. John's Abbey, Collegeville, MN
and meeting with Dr. Gregory Zilboorg.

THE TOWER OF BABEL, New Directions; poems. (play)
THE SILENT LIFE, Farrar, Straus; religion.

1958   THOUGHTS IN SOLITUDE, Farrar, Straus; religion.

1959   THE SECULAR JOURNAL OF THOMAS MERTON, Farrar, Straus; journal.
SELECTED POEMS, New Directions; poems.

1960   SPIRITUAL DIRECTION AND MEDITATION, Liturgical
Press; religion.
THE WISDOM OF THE DESERT, New Directions;
religion.
DISPUTED QUESTIONS, Farrar, Straus; essays.

1961   Meeting with John Howard Griffin after years of friendly
correspondence. Awarded Medal for Excellence, Columbia
University. Photography started with Griffin's camera.

THE BEHAVIOR OF TITANS, New Directions; prose
poems, essays.
NEW SEEDS OF CONTEMPLATION, New Directions;
religion.
THE NEW MAN, Farrar, Straus; religion.

1962   Meeting with Dan Berrigan.

ORIGINAL CHILD BOMB, New Directions; prose poem.

1963   LIFE AND HOLINESS, Herder & Herder; religion.
EMBLEMS OF A SEASON OF FURY, New Directions;
poems.
BREAKTHROUGH TO PEACE, New Directions; edited.

1964   Meeting with Dr. D. Suzuki in NY. Honorary L.D.,
        University of Kentucky.
        SEEDS OF DESTRUCTION, Farrar, Straus; essays.

1965   August 20, permitted to retire to hermitage.

        THE WAY OF CHUANG TZU, New Directions; philosophy.
        SEASONS OF CELEBRATION, Farrar, Straus; religion.

1966   Meeting with Jacques Maritain after years of intimate cor-
        respondence, when Griffin brought him to the Abbey.
        Meeting with Joan Baez, Sufi Master C.D. Abdesalam,
        Vietnamese Buddhist monk Nhat Hanh.

        RAIDS ON THE UNSPEAKABLE, New Directions; prose
        poems.
        CONJECTURES OF A GUILTY BYSTANDER, Double-
        day; notes.

1967   May 14, concelebrated Dan Walsh's ordination; preached
        homily.
        MYSTICS AND ZEN MASTERS, Farrar, Straus; essays.

1968   May, trip to Christ in the Desert, NM, Our Lady of the
        Redwoods Abbey, CA; early September and October,
        return trip to New Mexico, California, and a trip to Alaska
        for possible monastic site for a hermitage affiliated to
        Gethsemani (trip at the suggestion of the then Abbot at
        Gethsemani); spiritual workshop for nuns at Yakutat,
        Alaska. First trip abroad as a Trappist. Travel to India,
        Japan, Sri Lanka, Thailand. Addressed Spiritual Summit
        Conference of World Religions, Calcutta, India, and of
        Asian Benedictine and Cistercian nuns, monks, abbots in
        Bangkok, Thailand. Meeting with Dalai Lama, India.

        CABLES TO THE ACE, New Directions; prose poems.
        FAITH AND VIOLENCE, Notre Dame; essays.
        ZEN AND THE BIRDS OF APPETITE, New Directions;
        essays.

        December 10, death in Bangkok.

        December 17, burial at the Abbey of Gethsemani, Trap-
        pist, KY.

109

Notes on Contributors

WALMIR AYALA: Argentine poet, journalist, art critic.

JOAN BAEZ: singer; activist; author of *Daybreak*, an autobiography.

SISTER MARY ANTHONY BARR: Dominican nun; teacher at St. Cecilia
Academy-at-Overlook, Nashville, Tennessee.

ELZA BEBIANNO: Argentine poet, writer.

DANIEL BERRIGAN: poet; priest; author of *The World for
Wedding, Selected and New Poems, Prison Poems*.

WENDELL BERRY: poet; novelist; farmer; author of *The Broken
Ground, Findings, Clearing, A Continuous Harmony: Essays
Cultural and Agricultural*.

ERNESTO CARDENAL: poet; priest; Minister of Culture in Nicaragua;
author of *Zero Hour and Other Documentary Poems, The
Gospel in Solentiname*.

MARK VAN DOREN: poet; writer; critic; professor; author of *Selected
Poems, Autobiography, The Shining Place*.

CHARLES DUMONT: Cistercian monk at the Monastery of Scourmont,
Belgium; chief editor, *Collectanea Cisterciensia*.

JONATHAN GREENE: poet; founder and editor of Gnomon Press,
Frankfort, Kentucky; author of *Scaling the Walls, Peripatetics*.

MIGUEL GRINBERG: poet; writer; editor of *Mutantia*, Buenos Aires,
Argentina.

GOPAL HONNALGERE: poet, teacher, author of several volumes of poetry published in India.

VINTILA HORIA: Rumanian-born writer now living in Paris and writing in French; Prix Goncourt winner for his novel, *God Was Born in Exile*.

ANN JONAS: widely published poet from Louisville, Kentucky; publications in *Southern Review, Colorado Quarterly, Prism International, The Diamond Anthology* and Merton's *Monks Pond*.

JACK KEROUAC: author of *On the Road, The Dharma Bums, Mexico City Blues, Book of Dreams*.

ROBERT LAX: poet; close friend of Merton; their exchange of letters published under the title, *A Catch of Anti-Letters*; also author of *Fables, The Circus of the Sun*.

SISTER THÉRÈSE LENTFOEHR: member of the Congregation of the Sisters of the Divine Savior; poet; critic; author of *Now There Is Beauty, Moment in Ostia, Words and Silence: On the Poetry of Thomas Merton*.

JULIUS LESTER: novelist; journalist; author of *To Be a Slave, Searching for a New Land, Revolutionary Notes*.

ALLEN DE LOACH: poet; professor; author of *From Maine, Third Part Unordered*.

CORA LUCAS: poet; publications in *Wind, Pegasus, Adena*; wife of Merton's physician in Louisville.

T. R. MCCLELLAN: writer from Texas.

CARMEN DE MELLO: Argentine poet; translator of Merton's poetry into Portuguese under the title, *Vinho Do Silencio*.

JOEL P. MIRABUENO: Filipino poet, author of *Like a Nightingale*.

MICHAEL MOTT: Merton's official biographer; now teaches at Bowling Green University; author of *The Helmet and Wasp* and *Absence of Unicorns, Presence of Lions*.

JAMES NICHOLAS: Welsh poet, writer, critic.

BROTHER PATRICK RYAN: Cistercian at the Abbey of Genesee, Piffard, New York; teacher of theology and monastic studies at the Abbey.

RON SEITZ: poet; professor at Bellarmine College, Louisville, Kentucky.

FRANCIS SWEENEY: Jesuit priest, poet.

ARMINDO TREVISAN: poet; critic; professor of art history and aesthetics; winner of the Brazilian Authors Guild's Goncalves Dias National Prize for Poetry.

JONATHAN WILLIAMS: poet; founder/director of The Jargon Society, North Carolina; author of *Elegies and Celebrations, Selected Poems, 1957-1967, Elite/Elate Poems: Poems 1971-1975.*